CHARACTER
STRENGTH

ZEST

Sara Antill

PowerKiDS
press
New York

Published in 2014 by The Rosen Publishing Group, Inc.
29 East 21st Street, New York, NY 10010

First Edition

Editor: Jennifer Way
Book Design: Greg Tucker

Photo Credits: Cover, p. 6 Compassionate Eye Foundation/Taxi/Getty Images; p. 4 Stephanie de Sakutin/AFP/Getty Images; p. 5 Jupiterimages/Brand X Pictures/Thinkstock; p. 7 Elsa/Getty Images; p. 8 Jeff Cadge/Photographer's Choice/Getty Images; p. 9 Lian Deng/Shutterstock.com; p. 10 iStockphoto/Thinkstock; p. 11 Tibrina Hobson/FilmMagic/Getty Images; p. 12 © Bettmann/Corbis/AP Images; p. 13 Silver Screen Collection/Moviepix/Getty Images; p. 14 AFP/Getty Images; p. 15 © iStockphoto.com/Catherine Yeulet; pp. 16–17 Echo/Cultura/Getty Images; p. 18 Martin Valigursky/Shutterstock.com; p. 19 StockLite/Shutterstock.com; p. 20 Monkey Business Images/Shutterstock.com; p. 21 George W. Hales/Hulton Archive/Getty Images.

Library of Congress Cataloging-in-Publication Data

Antill, Sara.
  Zest / by Sara Antill. — 1st ed.
     p. cm. — (Character strength)
  Includes index.
  ISBN 978-1-4488-9677-6 (library binding) — ISBN 978-1-4488-9812-1 (pbk.) —
  ISBN 978-1-4488-9813-8 (6-pack)
  1. Enthusiasm—Juvenile literature. 2. Success—Juvenile literature. 3. Self-actualization
(Psychology)—Juvenile literature. I. Title.
  BF575.E6A58 2013
  153.1'533—dc23
                                          2012020307

Manufactured in the United States of America

CPSIA Compliance Information: Batch #S13PK2: For Further Information contact Rosen Publishing, New York, New York at 1-800-237-9932

Contents

STRENGTHS FOR SUCCESS

What does being successful mean to you? To some, it means getting good grades in school. To others, it might mean doing well in sports or going to college. Everyone wants to be successful and reach his goals.

Although people have different goals, those who succeed share many character strengths, or strong parts of their **personalities**. One of these important

Oprah Winfrey (1954-)

Oprah Winfrey is best known as a talk show host. She **encouraged** zest in her viewers by challenging them to "live your best life." Born very poor, Winfrey became one of the richest and most successful women in the world. She has donated millions of dollars to help people worldwide.

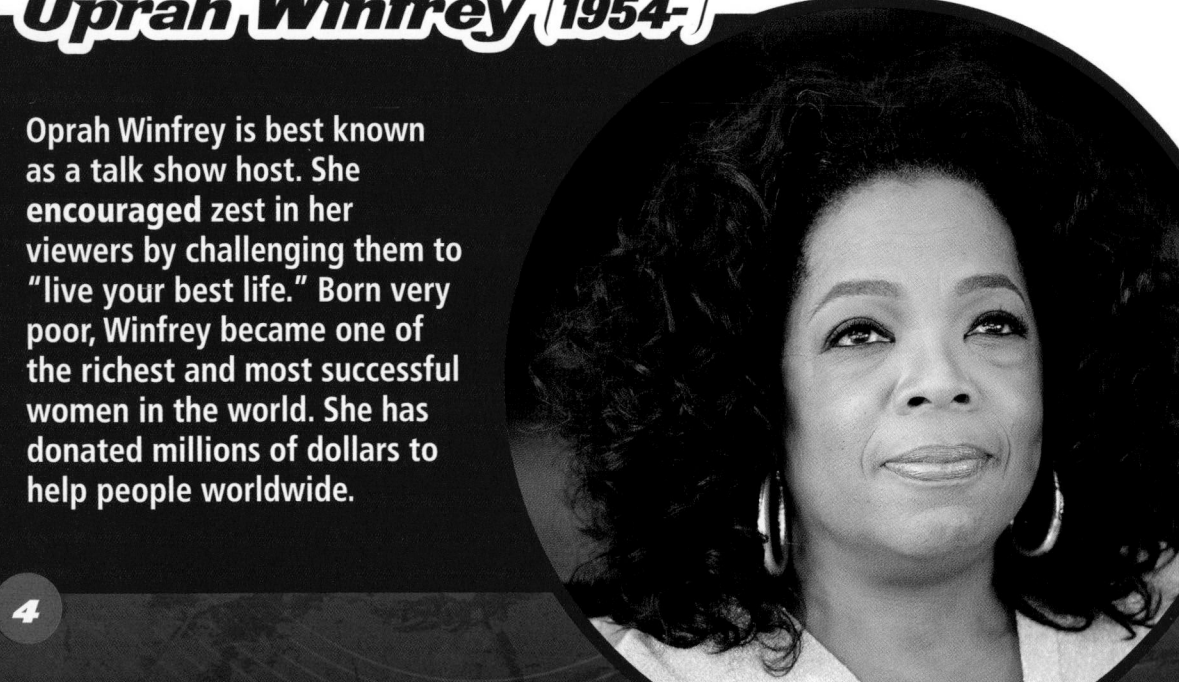

People with zest have good team spirit. They enjoy cheering people on.

strengths is called **zest**. In this book, we will see how living with zest has helped people be successful. You will also learn to find zest in your own life and in other people!

WHAT IS ZEST?

Do you know someone who always seems excited about life? When someone has a lot of energy and a positive **attitude**, or view, we say that she is living with zest. "Zest" is another word for "**enthusiasm**" or "spirit."

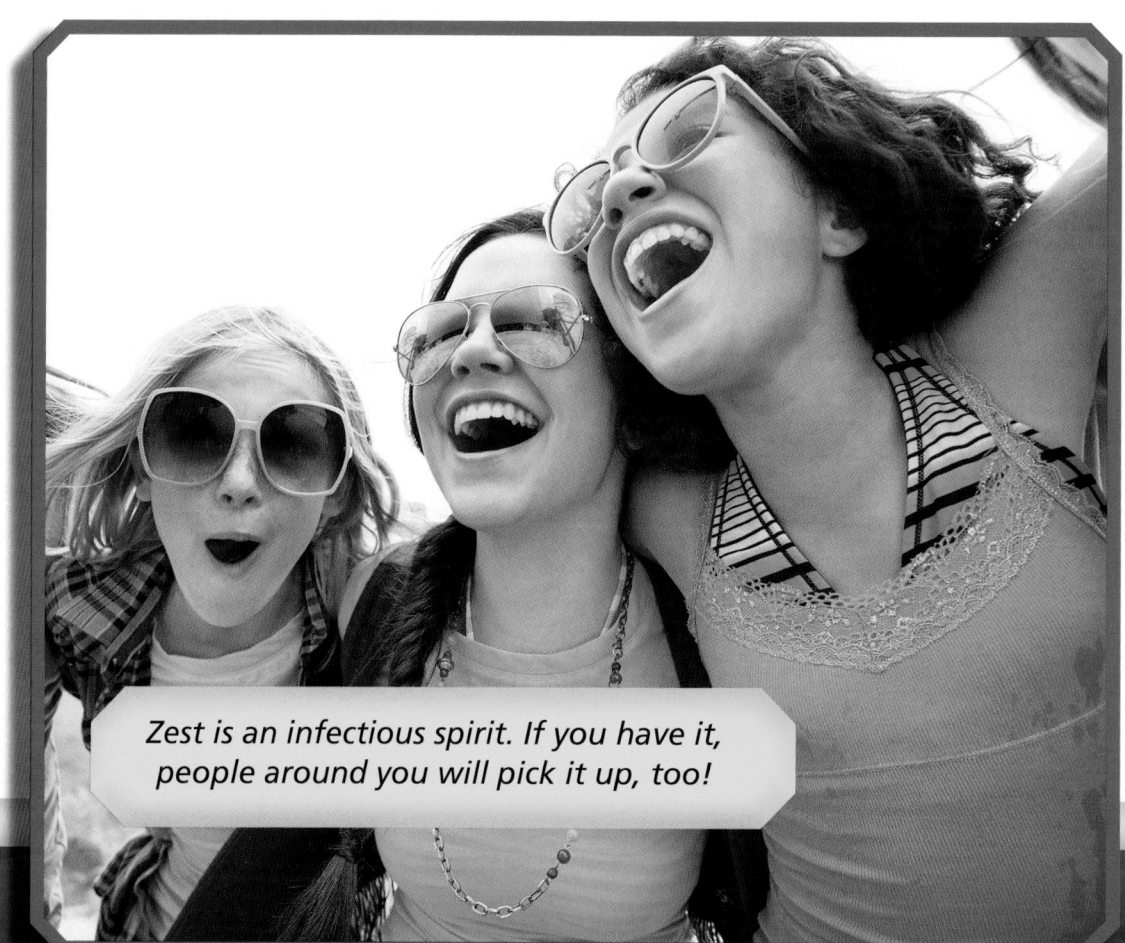

Zest is an infectious spirit. If you have it, people around you will pick it up, too!

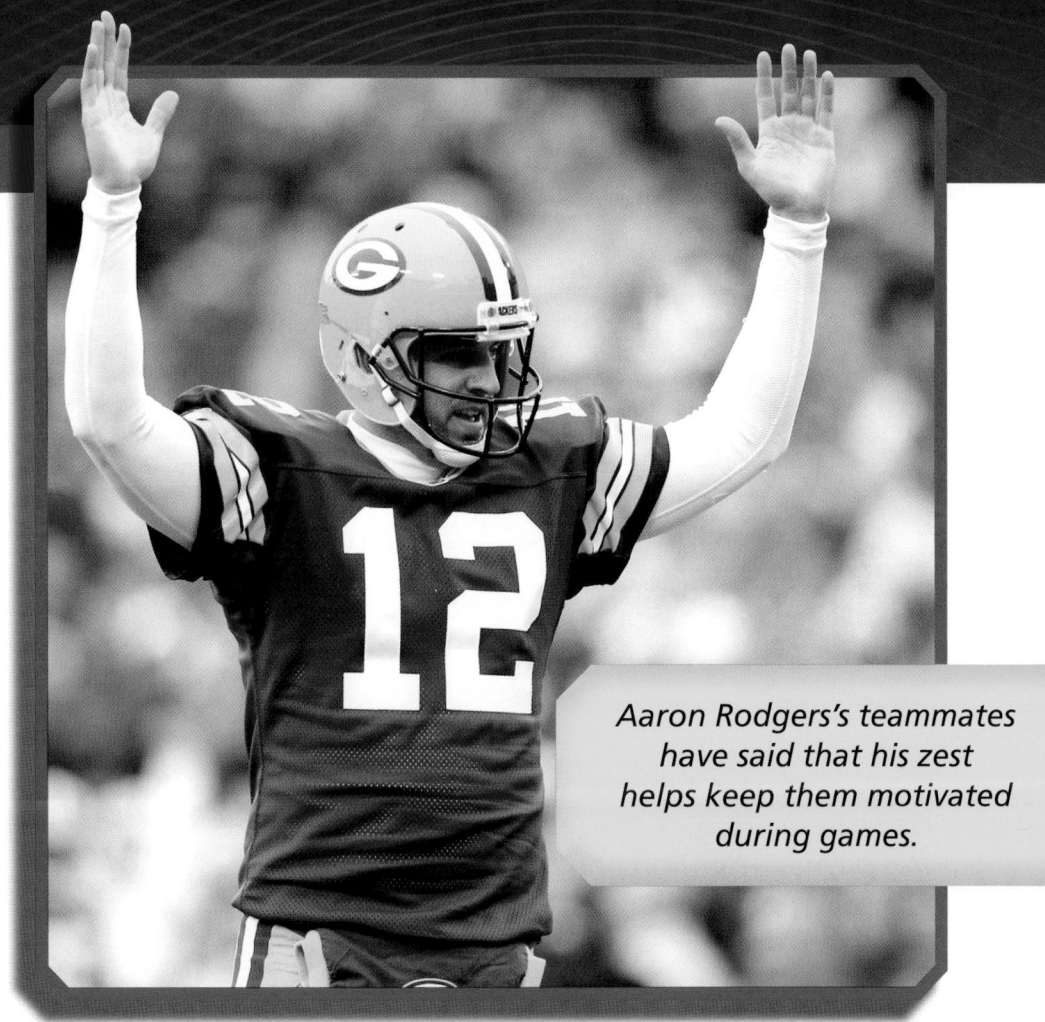

Aaron Rodgers's teammates have said that his zest helps keep them motivated during games.

Aaron Rodgers is a quarterback for the Green Bay Packers football team. He is known for the "Championship Belt" dance he does when he scores a touchdown. It gets his teammates and Green Bay Packers fans excited. Rodgers's zest is so infectious that this dance has spread to players from other teams!

A person with zest likes challenges. In school, a student with zest might raise her hand to answer a math problem or work on a special project for extra **credit**. To show that you have zest, you might try out for a sports team, even if you have never played the sport.

Being enthusiastic to participate in class requires paying attention and being prepared with your homework.

A person with zest might decide to learn to play an instrument and join the school band. This activity is fun, challenging, and new to that person.

People with zest often take part in a lot of activities. This is because they love to try new things! They may not be good at everything they do. However, they learn a lot about which activities they enjoy and which they might be great at!

You can show zest by taking an active part in group projects. It is important to encourage the whole group to contribute.

SHOWING ZEST AT SCHOOL

Have you ever worked on a group project at school? You may have noticed that some kids sit quietly and let others do the work. Some kids, though, are ready to **participate**. They offer ideas and suggestions to help the group do a good job. These are the kids with zest! Does that sound like you?

Kids with zest are active listeners. That means they try to understand exactly what their teacher is saying. When they do not understand something, they are not afraid to ask questions. Their questions may even help others in the class who also did not understand.

Paula Abdul (1962-)

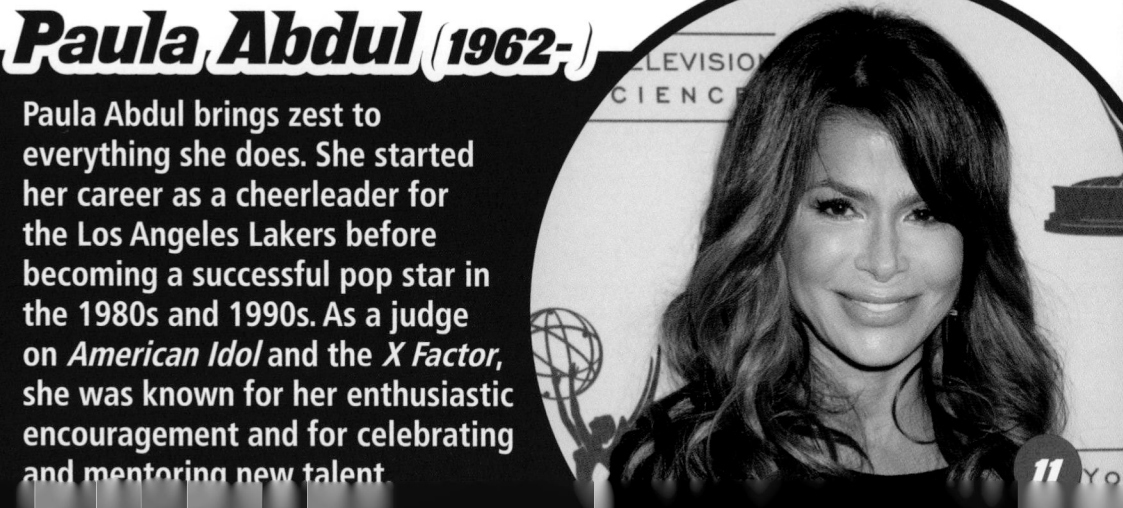

Paula Abdul brings zest to everything she does. She started her career as a cheerleader for the Los Angeles Lakers before becoming a successful pop star in the 1980s and 1990s. As a judge on *American Idol* and the *X Factor*, she was known for her enthusiastic encouragement and for celebrating and mentoring new talent.

ZEST ON THE PRAIRIE

Have you read the Little House series of books? They were written by a woman named Laura Ingalls Wilder about her childhood. In the books and in real life, young Laura and her family did not have an easy life. Her father was a farmer, and his crops sometimes failed. Laura's family often had to move to new places.

Laura Ingalls Wilder lived from 1867 until 1957. Here she is signing one of her books.

Wilder's books were made into a TV series called Little House on the Prairie *that ran from 1974 until 1984. Melissa Gilbert, shown at right, played Laura Ingalls.*

Through all the moves, Laura kept a good attitude. Though she was always sad to leave her friends, she was happy that her family could stay together and begin a new life. Her positive attitude and zest helped her survive in hard times!

LOOK ON THE BRIGHT SIDE

Sometimes it can be hard to be enthusiastic about things you do not like. Whether it is a spelling test or moving to a new town, someone with zest looks on the bright side. Zest is an inner resource that helps you see the good things that other people may not see.

Brendon Ayanbadejo (1976-)

Brendan Ayanbadejo channeled his zest into a 2013 Super Bowl victory for the Baltimore Ravens. He also uses zest to inspire others in supporting marriage equality. He says that as a mixed-race son of parents whose marriage would once have been illegal, he is passionate about this cause. He writes and speaks out for of laws that extend marriage equality to all Americans.

When moving to a new town, a person with zest might be sad to be leaving old friends, but also excited to meet new people.

A spelling test lets you show your teacher what you know and what you need more help with. Moving to a new town gives you the chance to meet new friends by joining a sports team, **volunteering** at an animal shelter, or finding other fun ways to take part in the **community**.

FINDING ZEST IN OTHERS

It is easier to get excited about something when the people around you are excited, too. One person's zest and enthusiasm can spread to others quickly. Look around, and when you see people living with zest, let them know that you respect their good attitudes!

You can encourage zest in others by showing you appreciate their contributions. If someone asks a question that helps you understand something better, thank him for speaking up. Complimenting someone makes him feel good and increases his zest. That should make you feel good, too. Before you know it, you have helped spread zest throughout your class!

Giving others credit for their contributions and showing that you appreciate their work are good ways to encourage zest in your classmates.

GROWING YOUR ZEST

Not everyone starts life with the same character strengths. However, in the same way that you can practice kicking a soccer ball, you can practice having zest. Take a moment to think about how much zest you show each day. Now how can you improve and show even more?

Zest takes practice. You might give yourself a goal to try a new thing, such as joining a soccer team. Then you can get excited about learning a new sport.

Volunteering to speak in front of your social studies class shows that you care about understanding the subject. Your zest shows that you are taking an active role in your education.

There might be subjects in school that you find boring or hard, but you can work on growing your zest for those subjects. First, identify things that you are excited about, and then use that zest as fuel. Finding things you are passionate about will help you approach things that frustrate or challenge you with greater zest.

A new project is often fun at the very beginning and easy to get excited about. Zest helps you get started, but grit will help you see the project to the end.

BALANCING YOUR STRENGTHS

When you live with zest, you are giving yourself a better chance to succeed. It is important to **balance** your zest with other strengths, too. Kids with zest get excited about new things. However, getting excited does not always help you finish a project if you give up when things get hard. Sticking with something even when it is hard is called **grit**.

Kids with zest also like to share their ideas. You may get so excited, though, that you do not give others a chance to share their ideas. Remember, a big part of living with zest is being a good listener and getting excited about what you learn!

Edmund Hillary (1919-2008) and Tenzing Norgay (1914-1986)

Edmund Hillary (right) and his Nepali guide Tenzing Norgay (left) were the first people to reach the top of Mount Everest, the tallest mountain on Earth. Though shy as a kid, Hillary became excited about adventure through books. After climbing Mount Everest, Hillary helped the people of Nepal by building hospitals and schools.

MY REPORT CARD: ZEST

How much zest do you show each day? On a separate sheet of paper, count how many items on the following list sound like you. Be honest about your answers! If you are not happy with your zest score, do not be upset. Practice living with zest for a few days or weeks, and then take the test again.

☐ I participate actively in class.

☐ I ask for help when I need it.

☐ I try to get others excited about the things I like.

☐ I listen closely to what other people say.

☐ I am willing to try new things.

☐ I encourage others to speak up.

☐ I give others credit when they do a good job.

☐ I am excited to learn new things.

☐ I am not afraid to ask questions.

☐ I know I can succeed if I try hard.

Glossary

attitude (AH-tih-tood) A person's outlook or position in a situation.

balance (BAL-ens) To have the right mix of things.

community (kuh-MYOO-nih-tee) A place where people live and work together.

credit (KREH-dit) The honor that someone who does something special gets.

encouraged (in-KUR-ijd) Gave hope, cheer, or certainty.

enthusiasm (in–THOO-zee-a-zum) An eager interest in doing something.

grit (GRIT) Showing courage in the face of hardship.

participate (par-TIH-suh-payt) To take part in something.

personalities (per-sun-A-lih-teez) Individual qualities that make people different.

volunteering (vah-lun-TEER-ing) Working without pay.

zest (ZEST) Having high spirits and enthusiasm.

Index

Websites

Due to the changing nature of Internet links, PowerKids Press has developed an online list of websites related to the subject of this book. This site is updated regularly. Please use this link to access the list: www.powerkidslinks.com/char/zest/